HELP
CONFLICT

A Teacher with Chicken Feet!
[Don't look at the *feet*. Look at the *heart*.]
Are you tired of hearing troubling news?

Darlene Small

BOOKSIDE Press

BOOKSIDE Press

BookSide Press
877-741-8091
www.booksidepress.com
orders@booksidepress.com

Introduction

Being a teacher has made me more aware of conflict and violence happening each day not just in schools, but world wide. Conflict affects us every day on all levels.

Our students are facing a multitude of challenges, both personal and in the form of crime and violence that surrounds them. In these trying times, what they truly need is a spark of hope, a dose of love, a foundation of trust, authentic role models to look up to, and unwavering encouragement. Let's come together to provide them with these essential elements that can ignite their spirits, help them overcome obstacles, and inspire them to believe in a brighter future. With our support and guidance, we can empower our students to navigate their way through these difficulties and find the strength within themselves to thrive.

In sports I noticed the quarterback doesn't always agree with the coach's call. Nevertheless, sometimes they win and sometimes they lose, but at the end of the game, they go over to share and give handshakes to each other. In so doing, that lets me know conflict can be acknowledged. The world can come together for sports, why can't we come together for the sake of our children.

I am sharing my thoughts, especially for teachers, parents and others to help alleviate conflict. However, if we think before reacting to make the right decisions, we would be making a huge difference to alleviate the sufferings in our world today.

From an educator's point of view, one of the greatest losses we have suffered is the old-fashioned dinner hour. Years ago, the family would gather around the dinner table basking in the warmth of love, warmth of peace, conversing, and watching each other's reactions. They would sit there for hours talking about their day, school, family and what's going on in the world.

When bedtime came, it seemed like the natural thing to do was to get a good book and read without media. Naturally, a good night's sleep followed and the next day minds were clear and serene. Out of such life came what we called "table side manners," which help with calming conflict. We need togetherness where we can get to the root of things that trouble us.

I think because of our materialistic goals, "trying to keep up with the Joneses," and the "let's make a deal" mentality, our children see right through us. Our youth are crying out to us to do something, they are disengaged, disenchanted, disillusioned, dishonored, discontented, disconnected, discouraged, disappointed, disarrayed, and full of disbelief.

In homes, many of our youth are living with a lot of negative conflicts. Parents question why their children are so little interested in school and ready to give up on education. They wonder why it is so difficult to reach their children with the concept of academic excellence. We don't see that our own example can be a stumbling block to our child's emotional development.

Doing right is not an inherited tendency. It does not come to us by accident. It is taught by leadership and example. It is earned by individual efforts, through the merits of a divine example.

Self-control is learned individually. It is formed by hard serious battles with self. The possibilities lie with our will. The company we keep, the habits we form, and the principles we adopt will affect our will. Let no excuse cause you to make a wrong decision to lead someone in the wrong direction.

Things that help our children:

> ➤ our time
> ➤ our influence
> ➤ our health
> ➤ our talents
> ➤ our manners
> ➤ our genuine love
> ➤ our commitment
> ➤ our truthfulness
> ➤ our communication
> ➤ our right example
> ➤ our integrity
> ➤ our devotion
> ➤ our respect
> ➤ our self-control
> ➤ our spending time in nature

Just know "an ounce of prevention" dealing with conflict and self-control on a regular basis at home promotes a sweet disposition in classrooms. It helps with teachers smoothing out disruptions.

One youth, in particular, was a real struggle because she brought all of her childhood anger to my class. The things I had learned from college, just did not seem to work for this particular child. She challenged me and had excuses for all her behaviors. I had to give her space to talk, rearrange my classroom, change my tone of voice, get to know her family, and show her real compassion. It took six months to establish a rapport with her and finally, she was manageable. It's been years, nevertheless, she taught me more than a degree. She has graduated from college and making a positive role in society.

Dedicated teachers should not be satisfied with just teaching students technical knowledge. We need to inspire our students with principles of truth, honesty, obedience, honor, purity, integrity, self-control, and trust that will make a positive stimulus in this unstable world.

Some statements students don't want to hear:

> ➢ troublemaker
> ➢ shut up
> ➢ get out of my face
> ➢ good-for-nothing
> ➢ I wish you weren't born
> ➢ you are just like your daddy/mommy

Our daily lives are determining the way we handle differences of opinion. Conflict begins at birth and continues to the grave. We should give our children a precious living example of what we desire them to be.

When you react to conflict, always remember that consequences come with the actions you choose:

➢ Disagreements can directly affect one's ability to properly solve problems and make good decisions.

➢ Erraneous of opinions can rob a person of their natural abilities and talents.

➢ Disputes can hinder team building efforts.

➢ Squabbles can arise when people compete and focus on self.

➢ Quarrels can and lead to explosive situations with deadly results that you wish you could change.

➢ Frictions can change a happy occasion into an unhappy episode.

➢ Dissension can turn friends into enemies and families into strangers.

The common conflict that we face daily is the battle we have with ourselves. Think of the many times you have struggled within yourself over a decision that you had to make. How many times did you wish you would have done it differently?

Oh, I must be fair and state that some forms of conflict can be positive, healthy, and worthwhile. Some differences of opinion can positively alter a decision, and change attitudes or behaviors. Unfortunately, it is the negative conflict that remains a noteworthy topic to research. I challenge you to do some research on what happens when negative conflict takes over a mind.

As a professional teacher, I have noticed a growing number of negative conflicts and tension-filled environments. Teachers are doing more mediation and conflict resolution than teaching. I am very much concerned about our teachers echoing the same issue. I googled school shootings in the USA since 1970, I found 2,069 and the numbers are increasing. Eighteen school shootings have taken place so far in the year 2023.

These are some of the reasons students give for their negative behavior:

- one parent family
- lack of communication
- too much social media
- attitude
- no genuine love
- no commitment
- no respect
- no backbone to rules
- no quality time together with family
- selfishness
- loss of respect for leaders
- no morals
- no integrity
- no devotional time
- greed
- fussing and fighting in homes
- no real love
- no time for one another

In our homes, churches, schools and communities, we need to pledge individually to become all that it is possible for us to become, and to cultivate every faculty to the highest degree of self-control, so that we may do the greatest amount of good.

As an educator, these are some contributing factors that echo from our hallways and classrooms:

> ➤ lack of involvement
> ➤ lack of concern
> ➤ lack of discipline
> ➤ lack of human and divine love
> ➤ lack of commitment
> ➤ lack of self-control
> ➤ lack of stable relationships

One of the hardest things I had to learn was to hold my tongue after some major contention or harsh words were spoken to me. However, by reading the Good Book, I realized that there was power and assurance available to me. What a difference it made in my life, and for the best. Yet and still, if I fail, I shall not, I will not give up the struggle. I will resolve again, more firmly to be patient under every provocation. "Better to be patient than powerful; better to have self-control than to conquer a city." **Proverbs 16:32 (NLT)**

The Bible is giving assurance that the highest evidence of a man or woman is self-control. He who learns self-control rises above the criticism, put-downs, disputes, squabbles, disagreements, annoyances, and conflicts of which we are confronted with each day. "My dear brothers and sisters, take note of this: Everyone should be quick to listen, slow to speak, and slow to become angry." **James 1:19 (NIV)**

We should teach our students to think, and that jail is not where they want to be. We should teach this at an early age and it should start at home. Encourage hope.

H = Help with Handling
O = Our
P = Problems
E = Everyday

"Don't worry about anything; instead, pray about everything. Tell God what you need, and thank him for all he has done. Then you will experience God's peace, which exceeds anything we can understand. His peace will guard your hearts and minds as you live in Christ Jesus." Philippians 4:6-7 (NLT)

Count your blessings challenge!

Place a dime in the jar, when you know you held your peace instead of losing control.

(Who knows, you may become rich)

May we live our lives and have an anchor that when situations around us become discombobulated, irritated, confounded, confused, crushed, bewildered, rattled, or shaken we can hold on to our faith and pray like we did when one of our football players fell to the ground while playing.

The best book to have in your library is the Bible (the best seller). It can help people to pull together under any circumstances.

It helps me with my attitude toward people, situations, news, disasters, chaos, stress, and anxiety. Nevertheless, my side effects were more joy, peace, kindness, patience, self-control, and thankfulness. Try it out on a trial basis and see what it does for you.

Favorite texts from friends to help get started:

- John 3:16
- Psalm 34:8
- Proverbs 3:5-6
- Philippians 4:6-8
- Jeremiah 28:11-13
- Psalm 91:1-16
- James 1:2-5
- Galatians 6:9
- Proverbs 18:10
- Psalm 23
- Proverbs 17:22
- Matthew 5:3-16
- 2 Timothy 3:16
- Proverbs 17:28
- Jeremiah 29:11
- 2 Chronicles 7:14
- Psalm 37:23-24
- Philippians 4:13
- Psalm 139:23
- Proverbs 17:28
- Romans 8:28
- Habakkuk 3:17-18
- Psalm 32:8
- Numbers 23:19
- Psalm 62:8
- Philippians 2:5
- Jeremiah 17:14
- Psalm 27:1
- 1 Thessalonians 4:16-18
- John 1:29
- Genesis 1:1
- Isaiah 41:10
- Psalm 107:1
- 1 Peter 1:18-19
- Romans 6:6
- Revelation 3:11
- 1 Corinthians 15:51-58
- John 14:1-3

The use of my quotes
and
poems
are
greatly
appreciated.

PLACE THEM IN YOUR *HOMES, OFFICES, SCHOOLS,*
AND EVEN *THE WHITE HOUSE.*

HAPPINESS OR SADNESS TAKES ONLY

ONE PHONE CALL

ONE CHOICE

ONE DIME

ONE TRIP

ONE MARRIAGE

ONE NEIGHBOR

ONE JOB

ONE PERSON

ONE SECOND

ONE CHILD

ONE PLACE

ONE NIGHT

ONE STOP

ONE CONFLICT

ONE TIME

ONE WORD

ONE ACT

EVERYTHING IS CHANGING

Our government

Our constitution

Our laws

Our rules

Our morals

Our children

Our jobs

Our weather

Our environment

Our truth

Our love

Our ethics

Our conduct

Our standards

Our world

Our quality of life

Our money

Our country

Our borders

Don't Lose

Your Faith

Your Hope

Your Love

Your Morals

Your Respect

Your Patience

Your Manners

Your Courage

Your Truth

Your Mind

Your Integrity

Your Confidence

Your Commitment

Your Compassion

Your Smile

Your Self-Control

Your Sense Of Humor

KILLING IS A CHOICE

C = Choosing to

H = Hurt

O = Other

I = Innocent

C = Children on

E = Earth

PLEASE STOP AND CALL FOR HELP

REMEMBER: A PROBLEM CAN BE RESOLVED.

"The regret of a lifetime may be determined by your loss of self-control."

I walked into a store and noticed the line was long with only one cashier. I heard a lady's voice saying "next in line." What do you think happened? You probably guess right, everybody started to move to the other cashier, and the lady who was next in line went ballistic and a shouting match generated with a lot of unkind words.

De-escalating conflict is essential.

SHOW ME

SHOW A CHILD A BOOK
AND
HE MAY READ IT.

SHOW A CHILD A GUN
AND
HE MAY SHOOT IT.

SHOW A CHILD SOME DRUGS
AND
HE MAY TAKE IT.

SHOW A CHILD SOME FOOD
AND
HE MAY EAT IT.

SHOW A CHILD CRIME
AND
HE MAY DO IT.

SHOW A CHILD A GOOD LIFE
AND
HE MAY PRACTICE IT.

SHOW A CHILD FALSEHOOD
AND
HE MAY BELIEVE IT.

SHOW A CHILD SOME TIME
AND
HE WILL ENJOY IT.

SHOW A CHILD SOME LOVE
AND
HE WILL APPRECIATE IT.

SHOW A CHILD YOU REALLY CARE
AND
HE WILL THANK YOU.

QUOTES

"The man who can't live up to his word is like a car at an intersection not following instructions, confusion and pain."

"Most of today's conflicts can be found within the doors of our own home."

"A metamorphosis can take place in our lives, when we stoop down and help someone else in their nest."

"Approach life like a basketball game, enjoy the shots, make friends with your neighbor, enjoy the players and when the game is over, you get to go home."

"If the path of your footsteps is going in the right direction, then your footsteps are worth walking in."

"Your attitude can make all the difference between love or hatred and it will be seen in your actions."

"Today, I am looking for HOPE, not a drink."

"Things today are like gossip, by the time it gets around is not the same."

"One thing we all have in common, life, don't take it."

THE QUICKEST FIX FOR A CONFLICT
before you act foolish ----------- THINK

T = **TAKE TIME** to calm down

H = **HOLD** your peace

I = Say **INTELLIGENT** things if you speak

N = **NEVER** do anything you may regret

K = Be **KIND** and anger will melt away

WE ARE ALL TEACHERS IN ONE WAY OR ANOTHER

CONCLUSION

Aggressive behaviors are making our schools unsafe and learning more complicated. Problems in homes, schools, and communities are escalating. We have to put the physical safety of our students and teachers on top of the agenda. If you are not persuaded that conflict is an issue, read the newspapers, hear the news or look on social media.

I wish one individual along with another and another can make a difference. We need to free our educators to teach. We face the most unprecedented educational challenges in the history of our nation. I am reminded that change must start with me.

Ponder on this "if we trade our robe of foolishness for a robe of righteousness," we could help change the world.

"WDJSNU"

"WHAT DO JESUS SEE IN YOU?"

I HOPE THIS LITTLE BOOK
CHANGES A HEART TO LEAD AND
TO LOVE.
KEEP CLINGING AND HOLDING
ON TO YOUR CREATOR, BECAUSE
TOUGH TIMES ARE NOT FOREVER
ON HIS WATCH.
WE ALL NEED HOPE AND SOME
ENCOURAGEMENT.
BE GOOD TO YOUR FRIENDS,
FAMILY AND YOUR ENEMIES
AND SHARE THIS BOOK.

Darlene Small
My Autograph to you.

NOTES/EXAMPLES

Economy is unstable.

Houses, apartments and food prices are steadily going up.

Banks are failing us.

Weather is unpredictable.

Turbulence by land, air and sea.

We are having conflict with just plain intelligence, now we have artificial intelligence.

Let's make the world a better place to live in.

Pride, greed and selfishness closes the door for others to walk in peacefully.

Your life is a reflection of what's in your heart.

Four things we should never lose, our peace, our hope, our honesty and our Love.

Four things that can destroy us, our lust, our pride, our anger, and our greed.

Ephesians 4:31-32 (KJV) Let all bitterness, and wrath, and anger, and clamour, and evil speaking, be put away from you, with all malice:

And be ye kind one to another, tenderhearted, forgiving one another, even as God for Christ sake hath forgiven you.

NOTES

NOTES